THE CALABASH
Abner Nyamende

The upper end of a fireplace
is its permanent seat.
Round-bellied it presides over family issues;
and from its regal seat
watches the newly-wed bride about her morning chores.
It is reassurance to the young and the old,
that there will be food, always, in this house.
Cats and dogs swear by it, and claim it's fed them well till now.
Where it sits, away from the doorway people can't;
and if they did we'd know in this home there's no custom.

In big homes they sit in a row
like judges sit to give sentence.
And unperturbed by the proceedings
visitors know there'll be food
and intloya for the thirsty.
Sometimes there stands one lonely, slender calabash,
To hold the little milk of one wretched cow or goat.
Then a neighbour's boy steals in and drinks it dry.

I saw it at a curio shop
and thought I'd buy it for my keeping:
a reminder of my childhood days.
And when I took it there arose the moaning voice
of a fly's desolate buzz inside,
trapped while hunting for scarce remains.

Abner Nyamende was born and grew up in the Eastern Cape. He writes poetry in Xhosa and in English.
He is a lecturer in the School of Languages and Literatures, University of Cape Town.

SOUTH AFRICAN
INDIGENOUS FOODS

A COLLECTION OF RECIPES OF INDIGENOUS FOODS, PREPARED BY **GENERATIONS OF WOMEN** OF THE REGION

REPRESENTING THEIR COMMUNITIES:
FREE STATE: M MANANZI, A THEBE
KWAZULU-NATAL: L HLOPHE, D NCUBE, P TEMBE
LIMPOPO: M MAIWASHE, E NDLHOVU, R MPHAFUDI
NORTH WEST: M MATLOU, J MOKWENA, S MOTAU
EASTERN CAPE: N VOVO, N Z MTYA, N KAMA

AUTHORED BY:
BOMME BASEMZANSI

COMPILING TEAM:
**TSHIDI MOROKA, LESEGO SEJOSENGOE, JANINE BARKHUYSEN
AND KGALADI THEMA – CSIR**

*Project funded by the Technology for Development Programme,
Department of Science and Technology*

Published by IndiZAFoods, Pretoria, South Africa 2004

First Edition 2004

Photographic credits:
Darryn Brooks (Pages 14; 16; 18; 20; 22; 24; 26; 30; 32; 34; 36; 38; 40; 42; 46; 48; 50; 52; 54; 56; 60; 62; 64; 66; 68; 70)
Dewald Reiners, Proshots (Pages 4; 6; 12; 28; 44; 58; 72; 97;104)
Loretta Steyn (Pages 5; 12; 28)
Lourens Uitenweerde, Eyescape Studios (Front cover photograph and pages 74; 76; 78; 80; 82)
Rudi van Aarde (Pages 2; 8; 44; 72)

Design and production: Loretta Steyn Graphic Design Studio – Pretoria
Printed by: Ultralitho

ISBN 0-620-31772-8

E-mail contact: info@indizafoods.co.za

DEDICATION

THIS BOOK IS DEDICATED TO
SOUTH AFRICAN WOMEN
FROM LIMPOPO, NORTH WEST,
FREE STATE, KWAZULU-NATAL
AND THE EASTERN CAPE,
WHO TAKE PRIDE IN THE TRADITION
OF INDIGENOUS FOOD PREPARATION.

ALSO NOTE ACKNOWLEDGEMENTS ON PAGE 99

**A LOCUST KEEPS FLYING
WITH A FULL STOMACH**

(YOU CAN KEEP GOING
IF YOU HAVE EATEN)

INTRODUCTION BY THE
MINISTER
OF ARTS, CULTURE, SCIENCE AND TECHNOLOGY

It gives me pleasure to present this recipe book of Indigenous Foods to current and future genera-tions of South Africans. Not only does the publication of this book celebrate part of the achievements of a decade of democracy, but also ushers in the next decade of innovations that combine indigenous knowledge and science and technology with the objective to improve the quality of life for all South Africans.

This recipe book is a catalyst in the fight against poverty and the use of indigenous knowledge in the founding of indigenous industries that create sustainable employment opportunities and also provide a springboard for our country to share our cultural heritage with the rest of the world. The book is but one of a plethora of products that continues to emerge from programmes of the poverty reduction mission of the Department of Science and Technology; namely, the organisation of rural women into a knowledge system that fights poverty, the establishment of a Section 21 company (IndiZAFoods) and the establishment of food production industries.

I recommend this publication as it preserves our indigenous livelihoods while giving the voice to rural women and illustrating their hitherto untapped expertise. It is my belief that as you explore these culinary treasures of part of South Africa, you will appreciate the potential that the rest of the country has yet to offer.

In conclusion, I would like to acknowledge and congratulate the successful partnership of the Department of Science and Technology, Communities and the CSIR.

Dr Ben Ngubane,
Minister of Arts, Culture, Science and Technology (1994 – 1996 and 1999 – 2004)

A MESSAGE FROM THE
DEPUTY MINISTER
OF ARTS, CULTURE, SCIENCE AND TECHNOLOGY

My department is proud to present to you this recipe book, which is but a glimpse of activities and involvement of rural women in the promotion of indigenous foods; a contribution to our heritage that is often overlooked or unappreciated.

The recipe book illustrates the vastness of traditional knowledge, often untapped and quickly disappearing, that could be harnessed and used as a vehicle for rural development that specifically empowers women, and in turn whole communities, given the pivotal role they continue to play in our country.

The successful compilation and publishing of this book illustrates the importance of support systems such as science and technology, business acumen and skills, training and literacy as well as access to affordable capital for women to establishment enterprises. The Department of Science and Technology, through the Technology for Development programme, optimally combines these incentives to drive its rural development initiatives within the Integrated Sustainable Rural Development and Urban Renewal Programmes.

The CSIR has successfully developed recipes that not only conserve and promote our rich heritage but also adapted them to modern food production systems and processes that use readily available ingredients to produce wholesome and nutritious products. Each recipe is a contribution by people of a particular region of South Africa, sharing their cultural specialities with the rest of the country by providing a rich tapestry of culinary experiences that we are proud to share with the rest of the world.

I invite you to celebrate with our people in saying:
Tsie e fofa ka moswang
Amathanga ahlanzela abangenamabhodwe
Imbiza yaziwa ngu mpheki wayo.
Tšie e fofa ka mošwang

Ms Buyelwa Sonjica
Deputy Minister of Arts, Science, Culture, Science and Technology.

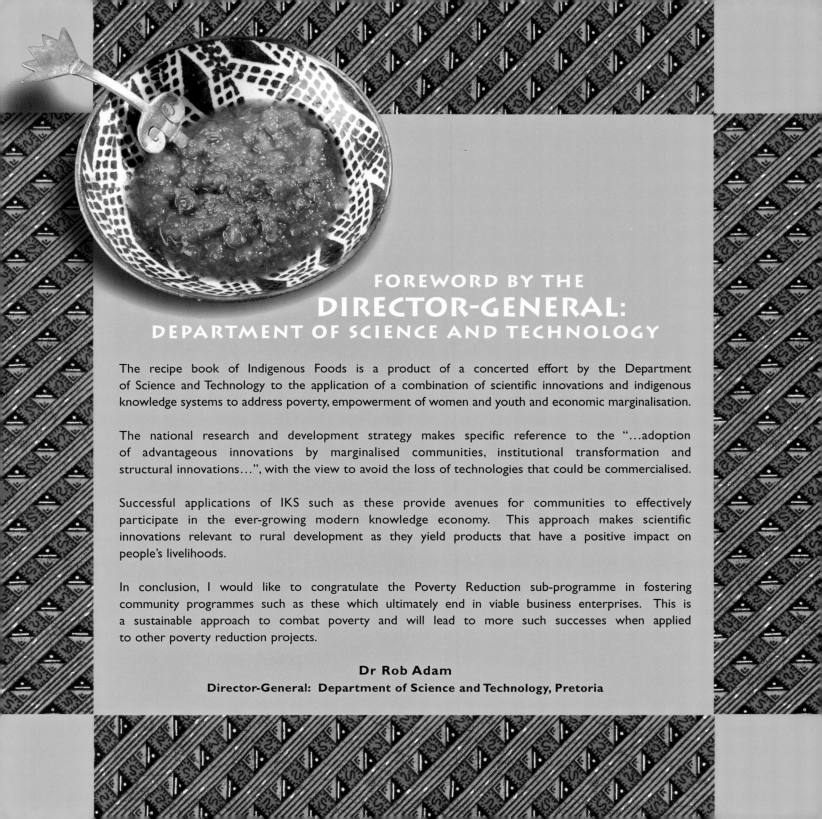

FOREWORD BY THE
DIRECTOR-GENERAL:
DEPARTMENT OF SCIENCE AND TECHNOLOGY

The recipe book of Indigenous Foods is a product of a concerted effort by the Department of Science and Technology to the application of a combination of scientific innovations and indigenous knowledge systems to address poverty, empowerment of women and youth and economic marginalisation.

The national research and development strategy makes specific reference to the "…adoption of advantageous innovations by marginalised communities, institutional transformation and structural innovations…", with the view to avoid the loss of technologies that could be commercialised.

Successful applications of IKS such as these provide avenues for communities to effectively participate in the ever-growing modern knowledge economy. This approach makes scientific innovations relevant to rural development as they yield products that have a positive impact on people's livelihoods.

In conclusion, I would like to congratulate the Poverty Reduction sub-programme in fostering community programmes such as these which ultimately end in viable business enterprises. This is a sustainable approach to combat poverty and will lead to more such successes when applied to other poverty reduction projects.

Dr Rob Adam
Director-General: Department of Science and Technology, Pretoria

Quantities

1 cup = 250ml
1 teaspoon = 5ml
1 tablespoon = 15 ml

*Recipes in this book
typically serve four
to six people*

Weights and volumes – approximate equivalents

Butter and margarine	250ml	250g
Dry beans	250ml	250g
Flour (bread, all-purpose, cake)	250ml	120g
Flour (whole wheat)	250ml	130g
Mealie meal	250ml	120g
Nuts, chopped	250ml	125g
Potatoes	2 medium-sized	250g
Salt	5ml	5g
Samp	250ml	200g
Sugar	250ml	200g
Tomatoes	2 medium-sized	250g

Names of Crops

Jugo bean / African ground nut (*Vigna subterranean*):
ditloo-marapo (Sotho); *izindlubu* (Zulu)
The jugo bean is indigenous to Africa. The colours of the seeds range from black to
spotted, yellow brown, red and cream.

Mealies / Maize / Corn (*Zea Mays*):
lefela (Pedi); *poone* (Sotho); *mavhele* (Venda); *ummbila* (Zulu); *mmidi / mmopo* (Tswana)

Tsamma melon / Wild watermelon (*Citrullus lanatus*):
lekatane (Tswana); Also called *lerotse*.
The wild watermelon is widely grown in Africa and Asia.

Sorghum (*Sorghum bicolor*):
mabele (Pedi, Sotho, Tswana); *amazimba* (Xhosa); *amabele* (Ndebele)

CONTENTS

RECIPES OF INDIGENOUS FOODS FROM FIVE SOUTH AFRICAN PROVINCES

FREE STATE

POTELE (Leafy vegetable and mealie meal)   **15**

SETJETSA (Pumpkin and mealie meal)   **15**

NYEKWE (Sorghum and sugar beans)   **17**

NYAKAFATANE-MABELE (Sugar beans, mealies and sorghum)   **17**

LEPU (Pumpkin leaves)   **19**

MOROGO (Indigenous green leafy vegetable)   **19**

MAQEBEKWANE (Steamed pot bread with bread flour)   **21**

MOTJAHAHLAMA/NTSEKANE/SENKGWANA
(Steamed pot bread with mealie meal)   **21**

NTSWAKANATSIKE (Steamed pot bread with sorghum meal)   **23**

DIRETLO/DIKAHARE (Intestines, tripe and lungs)   **23**

TSHOHLO/LEKGOTLWANE (Stamped meat)   **25**

SEQHAQHABOLA/MOTOHO (Fermented mealie/sorghum beverage)   **25**

MAHLEU/TSHWEU KOTO (Fermented mealie beverage)   **27**

SEBERA (Mealie snack)   **27**

DITHOTSE (Pumpkin seeds)   **27**

POTELE

(Leafy vegetable and mealie meal)

300g morogo, chopped, rinsed and
shredded
1 medium-sized onion, chopped
160g mealie meal
50g margarine
500ml milk
Add salt and pepper to taste

Bring milk to the boil. Add salt, shredded
green leafy vegetable (morogo) and onion,
reduce the heat and simmer for about
15-20 minutes. Add mealie meal and mix
well. Simmer for 15 minutes, stirring
occasionally.

Serve hot as a main meal.

SETJETSA

(Pumpkin and mealie meal)

560g pumpkin, cubed
165g mealie meal
50g margarine
500ml milk
Add salt to taste

Cook pumpkin and all other ingredients
except mealie meal for 20 minutes or until
cooked. Add mealie meal and mix well.
Simmer for about 15 minutes, stirring
occasionally until cooked. Serve hot.

Illustrated on page 14.

DO NOT GRIND THE MEAL
BEFORE THE MILKING HAS BEEN DONE

(NEVER BE TOO SURE OF A THING - FIRST THINGS FIRST)

NYEKWE

(Sorghum and sugar beans)

260g sorghum and kernels
200g sugar beans
50g margarine or butter
1 litre water
Add salt to taste

Wash and soak the sorghum and beans overnight. Bring water, beans and sorghum to the boil, reduce the heat and simmer until soft. Add margarine or butter and salt and allow to simmer for 3 minutes. Mash and serve.

Variations: Add 250ml diced potatoes, 250ml diced carrots and 1 small, grated onion, when adding the margarine and salt, and simmer for 10 minutes.

OR

Add 125ml sliced mushrooms, 5ml black pepper and 125ml fresh cream, when adding the margarine and salt, and simmer for 10 minutes.

Illustrated on page 16.

NYAKAFATANE-MABELE

(Sugar beans, mealies and sorghum)

230g sugar beans, cooked
190g yellow/white mealies, cooked
180g sorghum, cooked
15ml margarine
100ml water
Add salt and white pepper to taste

In a saucepan, bring water to the boil. Add all the ingredients and simmer until soft and cooked. Serve hot.

Illustrated on page 16.

LEPU

(Pumpkin leaves)

145g fresh young pumpkin leaves,
rinsed and chopped
460g pumpkin (small)
1 medium-sized onion, diced
1 medium-sized potato, diced
150ml milk
Add salt and pepper to taste

Cut pumpkin into small pieces. Place the
pumpkin leaves into salted, boiling milk,
reduce the heat and simmer for about
15 minutes. Add the other ingredients and
cook for another 15 minutes. Serve hot.

Illustrated on page 18.

MOROGO

(Indigenous green leafy vegetable)

90g morogo, rinsed and finely chopped
1 medium-sized onion, diced
250ml milk
50g margarine
Add salt and pepper to taste

Add all ingredients to milk and cook for
30 minutes or until creamy. Serve hot.

Variations: Add two medium-sized diced
potatoes and 30ml milk whilst cooking
morogo. Mash the potatoes with morogo.

OR
Add 20ml peanut butter instead of
margarine and simmer for 15 minutes.

OR
Add 30ml grilled and grinded pumpkin seed
powder (See page 27).

Note: Any of the 24 types of indigenous
morogo can be used.

Illustrated on page 18.

MAQEBEKWANE

(Steamed pot bread with wheat flour)

480g brown or nutty wheat flour
10ml dry yeast
10ml sugar
400ml lukewarm water
5ml salt

Mix the yeast with 60ml of the lukewarm water, cover and leave to froth for about 10 minutes. Sift dry ingredients.
Make a well in the centre of the dough.
Add the yeast and the rest of the lukewarm water to the dry ingredients.
Knead for about 10 minutes until the dough is elastic, adding lukewarm water as needed. Cover with a clean cloth and leave in a warm place to rise until double in bulk. Put in a greased bowl and cover tightly with a greased lid or paper. Steam for 2 - 2 ½ hours in a covered saucepan.

Illustrated on page 20.

MOTJAHAHLAMA/ NTSEKANE/ SENKGWANA

(Steamed pot bread with mealie meal)

335g mealie meal
275g brown bread flour
10ml instant dry yeast
10ml sugar
125ml boiling water
375ml lukewarm water
5ml salt

Mix the mealie meal with 125ml boiling water and leave to cool for 10 minutes. Add other ingredients and mix well, while adding more water if necessary and until the dough is elastic. Cover with a clean cloth and leave in a warm place to rise until double in bulk. Put in a greased bowl and cover tightly with a greased lid or paper. Steam for 2 - 2 ½ hours in a covered saucepan.

Illustrated on page 20.

NTSWAKANATSIKE

(Steamed pot bread with sorghum meal)

385g brown bread flour
160g coarse sorghum meal
500ml lukewarm water
12.5ml sugar
10ml instant dry yeast
5ml salt

Mix all the ingredients. Knead for about 10 minutes until the dough is elastic, adding lukewarm water as needed. Cover with a clean cloth and leave in a warm place to rise until double in bulk. Place in a greased mould and cover tightly with a greased lid or paper. Steam for 2 - 2 ½ hours in a covered saucepan.

DIRETLO/DIKAHARE

(Intestines, tripe and lungs)

500g intestines
500g tripe
500g lungs
500ml water
1 medium-sized onion
10ml pepper/curry powder
5ml salt
15ml vinegar/Worcester sauce

Wash meat thoroughly and cook in water until tender. Leave to cool and cut meat into small pieces. Add other ingredients to the meat and water and cook for about 15 minutes. Serve hot.

Illustrated on page 22.

TSHOHLO/ LEKGOTLWANE

(Shredded meat)

300g beef (on the bone)
200g mutton (on the bone)
500ml water
Add salt and pepper to taste

Cut the meat into chunks. Heat the water in a saucepan. Add the salt, pepper and meat, cover and cook until very soft. Separate the bones from the meat and sift the gravy. Use a wooden spoon to 'stamp' the meat. Add the sifted gravy to the finely stamped meat and simmer uncovered, stirring frequently, until the meat has absorbed the gravy.

Illustrated on page 24.

SEQHAQHABOLA/ MOTOHO

(Fermented mealie/sorghum beverage)

130g mealie meal or fine sorghum meal
12.5ml all-purpose flour
12.5ml sugar
2.5 litre water
750ml warm water
10ml dry yeast

Mix all the dry ingredients and 750ml warm water. Leave overnight in a warm and dark place to ferment. Bring 2,5 litres of the water to boil, add the fermented dough and stir thoroughly. Cook for 20 minutes, stirring occasionally. Serve either hot or cold.

MEAT WHICH IS FORCED INTO THE COOKING-POT BREAKS THE POT

(THE USE OF FORCE CREATES ILL-FEELING)

MAHLEU/TSHWEU KOTO

(Fermented mealie beverage)

75g mealie meal
12.5ml flour
12.5ml sugar
10ml dry instant yeast
2 litres water

Make a paste with 300ml cold water, mealie meal and flour. Bring water to the boil, mix with the paste and cook for 20 minutes. Leave to cool, add sugar and dry yeast. Stir well. Cover and leave in a warm place for 12 hours. Strain if it has lumps.

Illustrated on page 26.

SEBERA

(Mealie snack)

380g whole, dried mealie kernels
1 litre water
Add salt to taste

Cook mealies in water until soft but still chewy. Drain water. Reduce the heat and roast the cooked mealies in an iron pot or pan. Add salt to taste and serve.

DITHOTSE

(Pumpkin seeds snack)

500ml pumpkin seeds
Add salt and pepper to taste

Wash pumpkin seeds and grill in the oven for 10 minutes. Cool and season to taste.

Pumpkin seed powder: After grilling, grind into powder and add salt. Add to any vegetable dish for a good flavour.

KWAZULU-NATAL

MEALIE BREAD

335g ground mealies ('doughy' consistency)
130g bread flour
20g peanuts, crushed
30ml butter or margarine
40g sugar
30ml baking powder
200ml milk
2 eggs
Add salt to taste

Grease an enamel dish or bowl with butter or margarine. Mix all the ingredients and put in the greased bowl. Cover tightly with a greased lid or paper. Steam for 2 hours in a covered saucepan. Serve warm or cold with meat and vegetables.

Illustrated on page 30.

ONE FINGER CANNOT PICK UP ONE GRAIN OF MEALIES

(RIDICULING A MAN WHO DOES MANY PIECES OF WORK AT THE SAME TIME, NOT MANAGING A SINGLE)

AMADUMBE AND SPINACH TART

Crust:
510g cake flour
140g amadumbe, cooked and grated
50ml milk
25ml margarine
10ml baking powder
5ml salt

Filling:
1 medium onion, chopped
60ml margarine
250ml spinach, chopped
200g grated cheese
1 egg, beaten
125ml sour cream or plain yogurt
Add salt to taste

Mix all the ingredients for the crust in a bowl and spoon into a prepared flan pan. Sauté onion in margarine. Blanch spinach for 5 minutes and drain. Mix onion and spinach with the rest of the ingredients for the filling. Spoon the filling on top of the prepared crust. Bake in a preheated oven at 180ºC for 30 minutes or until done. Serve sizzling hot.

Illustrated on page 30.

PUMPKIN SOUP

165g pumpkin, medium-sized,
peeled and cubed
50ml lemon juice
50ml milk
25ml sour cream
1 small onion, grated
1 beef stock cube and 500ml hot water
15ml butter
Pinch of white pepper
1 cinnamon stick
10ml salt

Heat the butter and fry the onion. Add the cinnamon stick, lemon juice, pumpkin and stock, and bring to the boil. Reduce the heat and simmer for 10 minutes or until the pumpkin is cooked. Add the milk, salt and pepper and mix well. Remove the cinnamon stick and liquidise the chunky soup in a food processor. Heat through, add sour cream and serve hot.

Illustrated on page 32.

ISITHWALAPHISHI

(Beans and mealie meal mix)

250g sugar beans
250g mealie meal
1 medium-sized onion, diced or sliced
500ml water
100g butter or margarine
Add salt to taste

Soak sugar beans overnight.
Bring water to the boil in a saucepan.
Add the beans, lower the temperature and cook over low heat until the beans are tender. Add the mealie meal and mix well, adding boiled water if necessary. Continue stirring until both the mealies and beans are cooked. In a frying pan, melt the butter or margarine and fry the onion until golden brown. Add the fried onion and margarine to the beans and mealie meal mixture. Mix well and serve hot with meat or vegetables.

ISIJABANE SEMIFINO YEZINTANGA

(Morogo and mealie meal)

250g mealie meal
700ml water
70g pumpkin leaves, washed
200ml milk
Add salt to taste

Bring water to the boil, add mealie meal and cook. Remove from heat when cooked. Cook the leaves separately in milk and add to the mealie meal. Add salt, stir well to combine and serve.

Illustrated on page 34.

ISIPHUPHULU SIKABHONTSHISI NAMAZAMBANE

(Mashed potatoes and beans)

500g sugar beans
500ml water
4 medium potatoes, washed and cubed
75g spring onion, washed and diced
15ml margarine
Add salt to taste

Cook the beans in water until tender. Add potatoes and spring onions and continue cooking until the potatoes are cooked. Add salt to taste and stir well to combine. Simmer for 5 minutes and serve.

Illustrated on page 34.

ISIJABANE SEMIFINO YEMBUYA

(Wild pumpkin leaves, pumpkin and mealie mix)

1 small pumpkin, cubed
140g wild pumpkin leaves
250g fresh mealies, crushed
2 chili peppers, finely chopped
750ml water
Add salt to taste

Bring water to the boil. Add pumpkin, wild leaves, crushed mealies and chili peppers. Cook until soft, stirring occasionally. Add salt and simmer for a few minutes. Serve hot.

IMFINO YEZINTANGA

(Pumpkin leaves and peanuts)

400ml water or milk
200g pumpkin leaves,
rinsed and shredded
150g peanuts, crushed
Add salt to taste

Bring water or milk to the boil. Add the leaves, reduce the heat and simmer until cooked. Be careful not to overcook the leaves. Add the crushed peanuts and salt to taste. Simmer for 15 minutes and serve hot.

Variation: Add 1 small, cubed pumpkin (skin and pips removed) to the water and simmer until almost cooked before adding the leaves.

Illustrated on page 34.

JUGO BEAN MIX

500g dried mealie kernels, cooked
500g jugo beans, cooked
500g mixed nuts
375ml water
Add salt to taste

Soak jugo beans and mealie kernels separately, overnight. Drain the water. Bring water to the boil. Add mealies and beans reduce heat and cook until soft, adding more water if necessary. Continue cooking. Grind the nuts, add to the mixture and continue cooking for a few more minutes. Add salt to taste.

IZINKOBE ZOMMBILA NAMAKINATI

(Dried mealies and peanut mix)

300g whole, dried mealie kernels
700g peanuts, crushed
1 bunch of spring onion, chopped
3 small chili peppers, chopped
375ml water
5ml salt

Bring water to the boil. Add the mealies, reduce the heat and simmer until mealies are cooked and very soft. Add the peanuts to the cooked mealies. Simmer for a few minutes. Add salt, spring onions and chili, and simmer for a few more minutes. Stir well and serve.

Illustrated on page 36.

INKUKHU YASEKHAYA NAMAQEBELENGWANE OMBILLA

(Zulu chicken and mealie dumplings)

1 whole chicken, cut into pieces and washed
335g ground mealies
500ml water
125ml warm water
70g cake flour
1 bunch of spring onion, diced
2.5ml baking powder
Add salt to taste

Bring 500ml water to the boil. Add chicken pieces, spring onion and salt. Meanwhile, mix the ground mealies in a bowl with 125ml warm water to make a dough. Form small balls by hand and flatten slightly. Add to the chicken, cover and simmer for 1 hour or until cooked. Serve with vegetables.

Illustrated on page 38.

YASEKHAYA EPHEKIWE

(Cooked chicken)

1 whole chicken, washed and cut into pieces
750ml water
1 bunch of spring onion, diced
1 medium-sized onion, diced
Add salt to taste

Bring water to the boil. Add chicken pieces, onions and salt, and leave to cook. Cook until tender and serve with vegetables and steamed bread.

SWEET POTATO SOUP

1 1/2 medium-sized tomato, diced
500ml sweet potato, cooked, skinned
and mashed
100ml mixed vegetables
25ml vegetable oil
400ml water
Parsley
5ml mixed herbs
Add salt to taste

Heat the oil in a saucepan, add the tomato
and simmer for 15 minutes. Add the sweet
potatoes, mixed vegetables, mixed herbs,
water and salt. Cover and simmer for 20
minutes. Remove from the heat, add parsley
and serve hot.

Illustrated on page 40.

UBHONYO/IZINDLUBU EZISEMANZI

(Jugo beans)

500g jugo beans, washed
625ml water
Add salt to taste

Soak jugo beans overnight.
Bring water to the boil in a saucepan.
Add jugo beans and cook for 50 minutes
or until the beans are cooked.
Add salt and mix well. Serve warm or cold.

THIS MATTER IS A POT OF SWEET POTATOES

(THE WORDS OF ALL MEN
POINT IN ONE DIRECTION: AGREEMENT)

IMBUYA/ IMIFINO SOUP

(Green leafy vegetable soup)

150g imbuya, chopped
250ml green pepper, chopped
1 medium-sized onion, chopped
1 beef stock cube
2 packets of beef soup powder
125ml fresh cream
500ml water
5ml salt

Bring 450ml water to the boil in a large saucepan. Add the imbuya, green pepper, onion, stock and salt, and cook for 15-20 minutes. Mix the soup powder with the rest of the water. Add slowly to the rest of the ingredients and simmer for 5-10 minutes. Liquidise the chunky soup in a food processor or press it through a sieve. Heat through, add the cream and serve hot.

Illustrated on page 42.

THE ONE WITH MANY HOMESTEAD SITES GROWS NO HERBS

(SAID OF A PERSON WHO IS ALWAYS MOVING FROM PLACE TO PLACE AND LIKELY NOT TO ACHIEVE MUCH)

NORTH WEST

TING YA MABELE

(Sorghum porridge)

420g mabele-a-ting/course sorghum
800ml lukewarm water
800ml boiling hot water

Mix the sorghum with the lukewarm water in a container. Seal it and place in a warm, dark place to ferment for one to three days – varying on the sourness desired.

To make soft porridge, add the fermented mixture bit by bit to the boiling water, stirring well to avoid lumps. Simmer on low heat for 25 minutes until cooked. Serve with sugar and milk as a cereal.

Add more fermented mixture to achieve a consistency thicker than soft porridge. Cook for a further 15 - 20 minutes. Serve with meat and vegetables as a main meal.

Illustrated on page 46.

TSHOTLHO YA KOKO

(Mashed chicken)

1.5kg chicken breasts, washed
60g butter
1 big onion, finely chopped
Add salt and white pepper to taste

Cook chicken breasts in water, reduce heat. Cook until the bones are separated from the meat. Drain any excess water. Separate the remaining meat from the bones and mash the meat. Heat the butter and fry onions until soft, but not brown. Mix with the meat and season with salt and pepper. Serve as a starter or with porridge and vegetables.

Illustrated on page 46.

JACKET SWEET POTATOES

3-4 medium sweet potatoes, washed and unpeeled

Place sweet potatoes in a cooking pot. Cover with water and cook until soft and tender. (Determine softness by piercing with a knife or fork). When ready, cut into slices and serve.

Illustrated on page 46.

BOGOBE BA DINAWA

(Mealie meal and mix of indigenous beans)

200g jugo beans
200g small brown beans (Dinawa tsa setswana)
180g mealie meal
1 litre boiling water
Add salt to taste

Wash the beans and soak overnight to reduce cooking time. Bring water to the boil, add beans and simmer until tender and cooked. Season with salt. Add the mealie meal to make a thick porridge. Cook for 15 minutes. Serve hot with meat and vegetables.

<u>Variation:</u>
Pour cooked, hot mixture into a dish and flatten it. Let it cool and slice into pieces.

Illustrated on page 48.

DITLHAKWANA

(Cowheels)

1kg cowheels, cleaned thoroughly
1 medium-sized onion, chopped
1 x 410g can of butter beans, undrained
Barbecue spice
750 ml water
Add salt to taste

Place the cowheels in a cooking pot, cover with water and cook until tender. Add the onions and cook for 5 minutes. Add butter beans, mix well and season with barbeque spice and salt. Simmer 5 minutes and serve hot.

Illustrated on page 48.

A FINE GRAIN IS ONE WITHOUT HUSKS

(A GOOD THING IS ONE WITHOUT ANY FLAW)

PATAS

(Fried potatoes)

4 potatoes, unpeeled and sliced
125g butter or margarine
80g all-purpose flour
3 eggs, beaten
10ml Barbecue spice

Cook the potatoes for 20 minutes (don't overcook). Leave potatoes to cool. Mix flour and barbecue spice. Dip potatoes in flour mix and then in the egg. Heat butter and fry potatoes until golden brown. Serve as a starter.

Illustrated on page 50.

DIPHAPHATA

(Flat bread)

500g all-purpose flour
5ml instant dry yeast
5ml sugar
250ml lukewarm water
Pinch of salt

Sieve and then mix dry ingredients. Add water slowly and knead until the dough is elastic. Cover and leave in a warm place to rise until doubled in bulk. On a floured surface, flatten small portions of the dough, and then bake it directly on a stove plate. Bake at high heat to turn brown on both sides. Leave to cool and serve buttered with tea or coffee.

Illustrated on page 50.

THE FINE CORN
IS EATEN BY THE OWNER

(IT IS FITTING FOR A HARD WORKER
TO GET THE BEST OF THE PRODUCE)

MOROGO WA LEROTHO

(Indigenous green leafy vegetable)

100g morogo, washed
1 tomato, finely chopped
1 medium-sized onion, finely chopped
150g butter or margarine
150ml boiled water
A pinch of salt

Bring water to the boil, add morogo, reduce heat and simmer until half cooked. Add onion and tomato and simmer until morogo is soft. Add butter and season to taste with salt. Serve with porridge and meat.

Illustrated on page 52.

POLOKWE

(Fresh mealie balls)

5 fresh mealie cobs or 370g sweet corn
125 grated cheese
5ml salt

Remove mealies from cobs and grind them until smooth. Add grated cheese, salt and mix. Mould the mixture into small balls and place in a creased bowl. Cover and steam for 50 - 60 minutes.

Variation:
Use ½ a cup ground nuts instead of cheese.

GEMERE

(Ginger beer)

5 litres water
50g packet of ground ginger
500g sugar
7.5ml cream of tartar
12.5g tartaric acid
Water

Illustrated on page 52.

Bring 1 litre water to the boil, add the ginger and simmer for about 10 minutes. Add the sugar and simmer for another 10 minutes. Pour into a 10 litre container and top up with the remaining cold water. Add tartaric acid and cream of tartar. Stir, leave to cool and refrigerate.

Variation:
Add raisins or pineapple with tartaric acid and cream of tartar.

SPINACH AND CABBAGE MIX

90g spinach, shredded
1/2 medium-sized cabbage, shredded
2 potatoes, diced
1 onion, chopped
50g margarine
Add salt and pepper to taste

Heat margarine and fry onions until golden brown. Add the spinach and cabbage and stir-fry for about 15 to 20 minutes. In a seperate saucepan, boil potatoes until soft. Add potatoes to the cabbage mixture, mash potatoes and season with salt and pepper. Serve with porridge and meat or with dumplings.

Illustrated on page 46.

MOTLOPI COFFEE

This is an indigenous coffee from a Motlopi tree's roots, which are dried and grounded into a fine powder and baked to perfection.

10ml motlopi coffee
1 cup of boiling water
Milk (optional)
Sugar (optional)

Mix coffee with boiling water and add milk and/or sugar if desired.

Illustrated on page 54.

KGOMODIMETSING TEA

10ml kgomodimetsing, dried
1 cup of boiling water
Sugar (optional)

Infuse leaves in water and serve with sugar if desired.

Illustrated on page 54.

SEMPHEMPHE PUDDING

(Wild melon pudding)

1 medium-sized melon
25ml sugar
250ml fresh cream
25ml maizena
30ml water

Peel melon and remove pips, cut into medium cubes. Boil the melon with a little water for 15 minutes or until tender. Drain the water, add sugar and fresh cream and thicken with maizena. Simmer and serve hot or cold.

MOSUTLHWANE

(Wheat and bean dish)

250g crushed wheat
125g sugar beans
15ml margarine
Add salt and pepper to taste

Soak beans overnight to reduce cooking time. Cook wheat and beans until tender. Add salt and pepper to taste. Add margarine and mix well. Serve with vegetables.

DITLOO

(Traditional African beans)

500g ditloo
(traditional African beans), de-shelled
2 litres water
Add salt to taste

Bring water to the boil, add beans and cook until tender. Add salt and serve as a snack.

THE BEAN BALLS ARE NIBBLED AT AS THEY ARE MOULDED

(IF TASKED WITH PREPARING FOOD, THEY CANNOT BE BLAMED FOR EATING SOME DURING PREPARATION)

LIMPOPO

MOROGO

(Watermelon leaves)

145g morogo (watermelon leaves)
200ml water
Add salt to taste

Bring water to the boil. Add morogo and salt and simmer until soft.

MABELE PORRIDGE

(Sorghum porridge)

400g Ting ya mabele (sorghum)
1 litre water

Bring water to the boil. Add mabele, mix well and cover. Simmer for 35 - 40 minutes until cooked. Stir frequently. Serve with meat and vegetables.

MPUNYANE

(Sorghum bread)

850g Ting ya mabele
750ml all-purpose flour
600ml lukewarm water
125g margarine or butter
125ml sugar
7.5ml instant dry yeast
5ml salt

Preheat oven to 180ºC. Mix all the dry ingredients. Rub in margarine/butter. Add lukewarm water and knead for 10 minutes. Cover and leave in a warm place to rise until double in bulk. Knead it again, place dough in a deep bread pan and bake at 180°C for 1½ hours until golden brown in colour.

Illustrated on page 60.

ONE DOES NOT PICK OUT TWIGS FROM THE MOROGO

(YOU SHOULD BE THANKFUL FOR HELP GIVEN BY A CHILD OR BY SOMEONE WHO IS STILL LEARNING)

DITHOTSE

(Pumpkin seed)

250g pumpkin seeds
25ml water
Add salt to taste

Place seeds, salt and water in a frying pan. Bring to the boil, reduce heat and simmer until all the water is absorbed. Fry the seeds until brown.

Illustrated on page 62.

KGODU

(Melon)

1 small-sized melon
250g mealie meal
10ml sugar
500ml water
Add salt to taste

Peel melon, cut into small pieces, cover with water and cook until tender. Add mealie meal, salt and sugar. Stir until cooked. Mix thoroughly and serve. Serve with vegetables or meat.

MOROGO WA DIMAKE

(Bean leave and peanut dish)

130g bean leaves, chopped
70g groundnuts or peanuts
Optional: chilies
Add salt and pepper to taste

Cover nuts with water in a saucepan, add salt and bring to the boil. Simmer for 5 minutes. Add chopped leaves and cook for 10 minutes. Add pepper or chilies to taste. Serve warm with porridge.

Fresh or dried bean leaves could be used, allow for a longer cooking time.

SMALL PUMPKIN, REMAIN IN THE MEALIESTALKS

(SAID OF A GIRL WHO DOES NOT GET MARRIED)

MOROGO WA BOVHOLA

(Pumpkin, pumpkin leaves and peanuts)

90g pumpkin leaves, washed and
shredded
70g pumpkin flowers, washed and
shredded
1 small fresh pumpkin
150g peanuts, ground
250ml water
Add salt to taste

Bring water to the boil, add salt, pumpkin,
leaves and flowers and simmer for
10 - 15 minutes or until pumpkin is cooked.
Add the peanuts and simmer for
5 minutes.

Illustrated on page 64.

MUTUKU

(Sour porridge with bran)

250g yellow mealie meal
500g fine white mealie meal
700ml water

Mix the yellow mealie meal, white mealie
meal and water, and leave to ferment for
2 days. Bring this mixture to the boil and
cook for 10 - 20 minutes. Simmer for
10 minutes and serve with meat and
vegetables.

Illustrated on page 64.

THE PORRIDGE IS LADLED OUT WHILE IT IS HOT; BUT BY TOMORROW IT WILL HAVE COOLED OFF

(EVEN IF SOMEONE IS ANGRY NOW,
HE WILL CALM DOWN LATER)

MASONJA/DHOVI

(Mopani worms and ground peanuts)

250ml mopani worms
125g peanuts, ground
2.5ml salt
750ml water

Soak mopani worms in hot water for
7 minutes. Wash it twice with warm water.
Bring water to the boil, add mopani worms and
salt and cook for 10 minutes or until water has
been absorbed. Add peanuts,
simmer for 5 minutes and serve.

Illustrated on page 66.

MAGEU/MABUNDU

(Fermented mealie and malt beverage)

75g mealie meal
750ml malt, grinded and sifted
200ml water

Bring water to the boil. Add the mealie
meal, mix and cook to a soft porridge.
Leave to cool. Mix with malt and leave to
ferment for 24 hours.

SHANGAAN (TSONGA) DISHES

TIHOVE

(Samp, beans, cowpeas, peanuts)

380g samp
250g jugo beans
250g cowpeas
62,5g ground nuts/peanuts
Add salt and pepper to taste

Soak samp, jugo beans and cowpeas overnight.
Boil the soaked ingredients until cooked (about
20 minutes.) Grind the nuts into powder and
add to mixture. Add salt and pepper to taste.
Reduce the heat and continue stirring for 15
minutes. Serve warm with vegetables or meat.

Illustrated on page 68.

XIENDLA HI VOMU

(Mealies, peanuts, dry beans)

350g fresh mealies
100g ground nuts/peanuts
250g dry beans
Add salt to taste

Put mealies and beans together in a
sauce-pan with water and boil until tender.
Grind the nuts and add to the mixture.
Add salt and pepper and simmer for
10 minutes.

XIGINYA XA MIHLATA

(Sweet potatoes and jugo beans)

3 medium sweet potatoes,
peeled and cubed
130g jugo beans
70g peanuts, ground
2.5 litres water
Add salt to taste

Soak the beans overnight. Bring water to the boil. Add jugo beans and cook until tender. Add sweet potatoes and cook until tender. Add peanuts, and leave to simmer for 10 minutes. Add salt, simmer for 5 minutes and serve.

XIGINGA XA MINTSUBULA

(Cassava and jugo beans)

4 medium cassava
390g jugo beans
250g peanuts, ground
3 litres water
Add salt to taste

Soak the beans overnight. Bring water to the boil, add cassava and jugo beans and cook until all the water has been absorbed. Add peanuts and allow simmering for 10 minutes. Add salt and mix well. Simmer for about 10 minutes and serve.

MABHACHA

(Whole, dried mealies and peanuts)

175g whole, dry mealie kernels
115g peanuts
25ml oil
Add salt to taste

Fry the mealies and the peanuts until golden brown. Add salt. Serve as a snack.

TINTSHUNTSHU

(Whole mealie kernels)

1.2 litre water
500ml whole, dry mealie kernels
Add salt to taste

Bring water to the boil, add mealies and cook until tender. Add more water if necessary. Add salt, mix well and leave for 5 minutes before serving.

XIRITSA XA TAMATI

(Tomatoes, onions and peanuts)

3 tomatoes, chopped
1 medium-sized onion, chopped
140g peanuts, crushed
25ml vegetable oil
150ml water
Add salt to taste

Fry onions in the oil, add tomatoes and fry until cooked. Add water and boil for a few minutes. Add peanuts and simmer. Serve hot.

XITOPYA

(Peanut dish)

325g peanuts, crushed
450ml water
Add salt to taste

Bring water to the boil. Add peanuts, mix well and simmer for 10 minutes. Add salt, simmer for 5 minutes and serve.

VUSWA BYA NWA-HUVA

(Millet porridge)

750ml water
1 litre millet flour

Pour 625ml water into a small bucket. Add 750ml millet flour, stir and leave to ferment overnight. Bring 125ml water to the boil, add fermented mixture and cook for 10 - 15 minutes. Add 250ml millet flour and cook for 15 minutes.

Illustrated on page 70.

TIHOVE

(Samp and peanuts)

310g samp
100g peanuts, crushed
930ml water
Add salt to taste

Bring water to the boil, add samp and cook until tender. Add the peanuts and simmer for 20 minutes. Add salt and mix well. Remove from the heat and leave for 30 minutes. Mix well and serve as is, or with meat or xiritsa xa.

EASTERN CAPE

QHUMATALA

(Sorghum and dry beans mixture)

260g sorghum kernels
200g sugar beans
50g margarine or butter
1 litre water
Add salt to taste

Wash and soak sorghum and sugar beans overnight. Drain excess water. Bring water, beans and sorghum to boil. Reduce the heat and simmer for an hour or until soft. Add margarine or butter and salt and allow to simmer for 3 minutes. Remove from the heat and serve hot.

Illustrated on page 74 and 78.

INKOBE

(Mealie snack)

380g dry mealie kernels
5ml salt
750ml water

Add the mealies to the water in a saucepan. Cook the mealies for 1½ hour or until tender. Add salt to taste. Remove from the heat and serve hot or cold.

UMXHAXHA

(Wild melon/pumpkin and mealies)

560g melon/pumpkin (1 medium)
165g mealie rice
50g margarine
25ml sugar
500ml water
Add salt to taste

Cook melon/pumpkin and all other ingredients except mealie rice for 20 minutes, or until cooked. Cook mealie rice seperately with water in a saucepan and simmer for 30 minutes. Add the cooked melon or pumpkin to the mealie rice and simmer for 15 minutes, stirring occasionally until cooked. Serve hot.

INTLAPHOYI

(Mealie bread with mealie meal)

660g mealie meal
300g bread flour
300ml boiling water
10 ml instant dry yeast
10ml sugar
Pinch of salt

Mix the mealie meal and the water and leave to cool for 10 minutes. Add the flour, salt, sugar and yeast and mix well. Knead the dough for about 10 minutes, adding luke-warm water as needed. Cover with a clean cloth and leave in a warm place to rise until double in bulk. Knead it again, put in a greased bowl and cover tightly with a greased lid or paper. Steam for 1½ hour in a covered saucepan. Add more water if necessary. Remove from the bowl and serve hot or cold.

Illustrated on page 76.

ISONKA SOMBONA

(Fresh mealie bread)

145g fresh or frozen mealies
30g all-purpose flour
2 eggs, beaten
25ml sugar
25ml butter or margarine
5ml baking powder
5ml salt

If using fresh mealies, remove the kernels from the cob with a knife. Mince the mealies. Add flour, spoon by spoon, to the mixture to form a firm dough. Add the eggs, butter, baking powder, sugar and salt to the mealies and mix well. Place dough in a greased tin and bake at 180°C for 1½ hour. Serve hot or cold with either meat stew or tea.

UMFINO

(Wild vegetables)

80g ihlaba
(wild spinach), chopped
80g umsobo
(wild vegetables), chopped
80g unqophose
(wild vegetables), chopped
80g mbikicane
(wild vegetables), chopped
900ml water
310g mealie meal
1 bunch of spring onions, chopped
60ml butter or margarine
Add salt to taste

Mix the wild vegetables and wash in cold, salted water. Drain and add vegetables to saucepan with 500ml of salted water. Simmer for 20 minutes. Add the mealie meal, spring onions and butter and the rest of the boiled water. Add salt to taste. Mix well and simmer for a further 20 - 25 minutes. Stir occasionally until well done. Serve hot.

ISOPHU YOMBONA

(Traditional mealie soup)

345g sweet corn
600g sugar beans
1 large onion, chopped
2 litres water
30ml margarine
Add salt to taste

Wash the beans and soak overnight in water. Drain excess water. Cook the beans. Add the corn to the beans and simmer for 1 hour or until the corn is cooked. Add the salt, onion and butter and simmer for a further 20 minutes. Serve hot.

CHOLA CHOLA TEA

Add chola-chola leaves to boiling water. Boil for 5 minutes. Serve as tea with sugar.

Optional: Add lemon juice and honey

UMPHOTHULO

(Ground mealies served with sour milk)

550g dry mealie kernels
1 litre water
500ml sour milk

Add the mealies to the water in a saucepan. Simmer for 30 minutes or until the mealies are slightly softer, but not fully cooked. Remove the mealies from the water, but leave the remaining water in the saucepan. Cool the mealies and grind. Remove the husks and add to the water in the saucepan. Simmer for about 15 minutes. Cool and serve with sour milk.

Illustrated on page 76.

UMNGQUSHO ONEMBOTYI

(Samp with beans)

380g samp
260g sugar beans
2 litres water
1 large onion, chopped
Add salt to taste

Wash the beans and samp and soak overnight in enough water to cover. Drain excess water. Add both to boiling water in a saucepan. Simmer for 3 hours, replenishing water when necessary, to obtain a soft, but not watery consistency. Add onion and salt and mix well.

Illustrated on page 80.

UQHAFUNYEKO

(Mealies with beans)

380g dry mealie kernels
260g sugar beans
2 litres water
Add salt to taste

Illustrated on pages 80 and 82.

Wash the beans and mealies and soak overnight in enough water to cover. Drain excess water. Add to 2 litres of boiling water in a saucepan. Simmer for 3 hours, replenishing water when necessary to obtain a soft, but not watery consistency. Add salt and serve.

MIXED FRUIT MARMALADE

10 oranges
10 lemons
5 grapefruit
2 litres sugar
4.5 litres water

Grate the peels from the fruit to get
1.5 litre of grated peel. Boil the water and
the peel. Simmer until the peel is soft.
Remove from the heat and leave overnight
(uncovered). Measure into cups and for
every cup of the boiled peel, add 1 cup of
sugar. Boil this mixture, spooning the scum
from the top as it boils. After about 1 hour,
the mixture will start to boil over. Drop a
little of the mixture on a cold saucer.
The marmalade is ready when a soft jelly
is formed on the saucer. Remove from the
heat and leave for about 10 minutes to cool
slightly. Pour into clean, dry bottles and
seal. After the product has set (about 1 day),
pour a little melted candle wax over the top
of each bottle to seal properly.

Illustrated on page 76.

LEMON DRINK CONCENTRATE

500ml lemon juice
2 litres sugar
12.5ml tartaric acid
12.5ml Epsom salts
12.5ml lemon rind, finely grated
1.5 litre boiling water

Mix all the ingredients and leave to cool.
Pour in clean, dry bottles and label. Serve
diluted.

Illustrated on page 76.

ISIGWAMPA

(Vegetables and mealies)

130g wild leafy vegetables, diced
2 medium carrots, grated
160g whole mealies, grinded
Add salt to taste

Cook the wild leafy vegetables for
10 minutes. Add grated carrots to the
wild leafy vegetables and cook for 5 minutes.
Add salt, mealies, mix well and simmer for
another 10 minutes.

Illustrated on page 82.

A PICTURE PORTFOLIO OF COMMERCIALISED FOODS

The Indigenous Foods Poverty Alleviation Project was commissioned by the then Department of Arts, Culture, Science and Technology and implemented by the CSIR. The project started with community interaction and traditional food preparation, and was followed by new product development, studies on stabilisation, food processing and shelf-life. Today these products are entering the market through a newly formed Section 21 company, IndiZAFoods. Some of these commercialised products are depicted from pages 85 - 93.

XANDO SNACK MIX

85

A PICTURE PORTFOLIO OF COMMERCIALISED FOODS

MARULA SALAD DRESSING

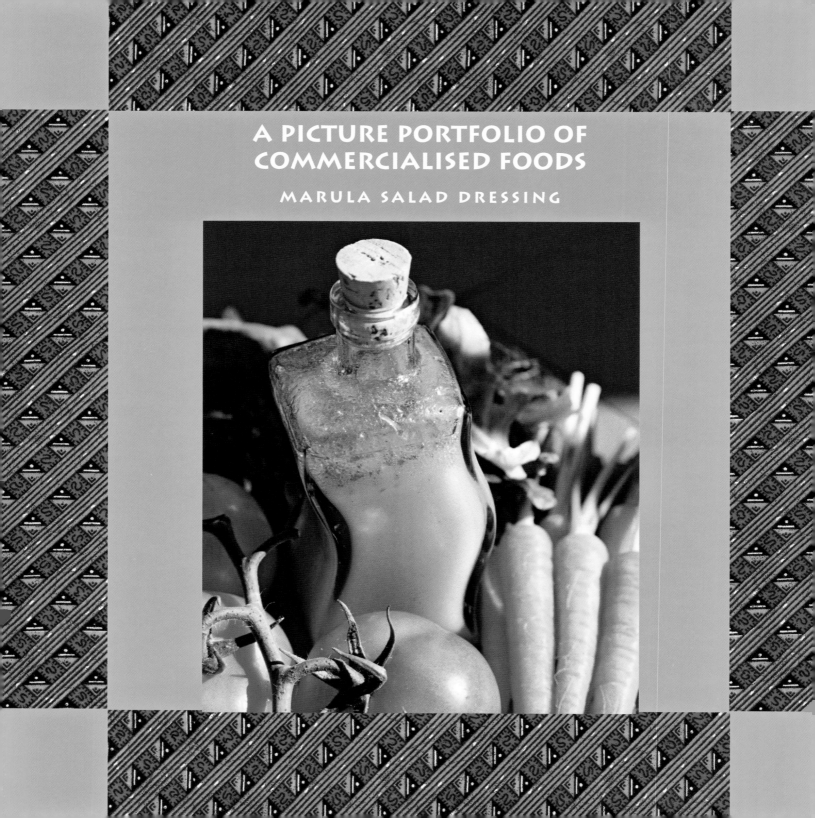

DIPABI CHOCOLATE BITES

A PICTURE PORTFOLIO OF
COMMERCIALISED FOODS

XIGUGU BISCUITS

AMADUMBE CRISPS

A PICTURE PORTFOLIO OF COMMERCIALISED FOODS

POTELE MUFFINS

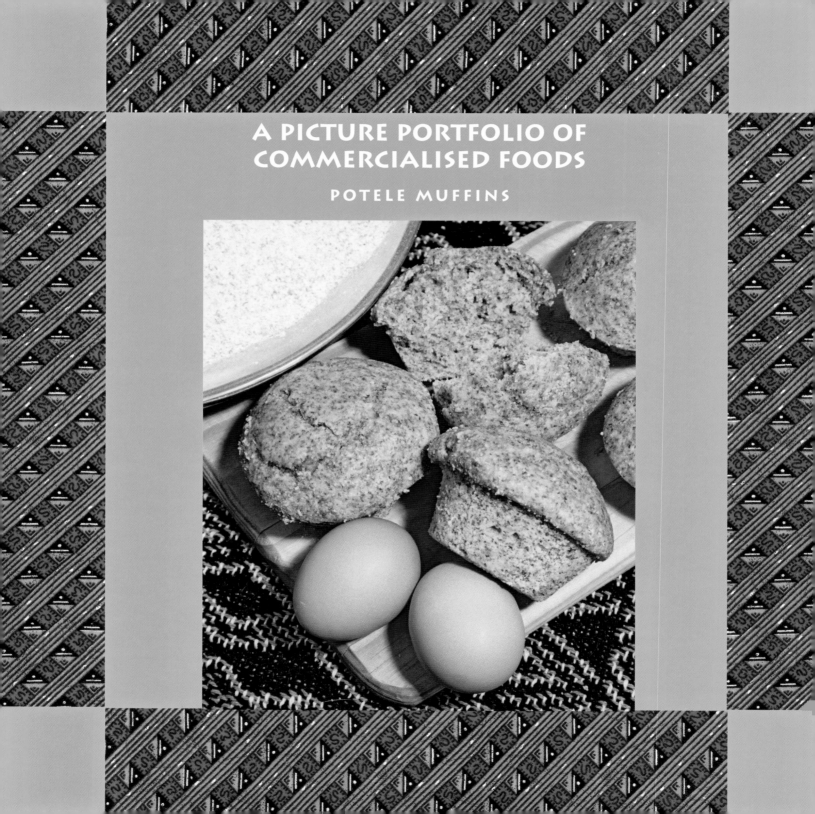

DIPABI BISCUITS

91

A PICTURE PORTFOLIO OF COMMERCIALISED FOODS

MARULA PINEAPPLE-FLAVOURED ICED TEA

MOHADIKOANE WHEAT PORRIDGE

**SWEET THINGS
NEVER FILL A SPOON**

(YOU WILL NEVER HAVE
ENOUGH OF A GOOD THING)

IN CONCLUSION

Tshidi Moroka,
Programme Manager: Technology for Development at CSIR Food, Biological and Chemical Technologies

Experiencing the pride of our country's rural women when flaunting their rich heritage in food preparation, has turned out to be one of the best experiences of my life. From the initial "…but who is interested in our foods?" to proud women who presented their foods at the lavish Provincial Food Fairs, have made for a wonderful project. Publishing a recipe book containing many of the recipes collected, is a fitting and tangible deliverable – one which hopefully will play a small part in both conserving and promoting our indigenous foods.

These recipes are like the people of the regions: simple, wholesome, close to nature and delightful! The main ingredients are those products that are readily available and typical of the area. Of course similarities occur in the dishes prepared in the various provinces, often with an additional ingredient that is abundant in a specific region being added to the composition.

The Indigenous Food Poverty Alleviation Project is primarily about commercialising indigenous foods, thereby contributing to alleviating poverty. Seeing children at a food fair scramble to get their hands on dipabi biscuits and chocolates proved beyond all doubt what potential lay hidden in our treasure chest of indigenous foods. Food scientists at the CSIR have added their speciality knowledge in food science and technology to create a product series for each province, and while we have opted not to include these recipes, hopefully, soon, you will be able to buy these products in stores. (As depicted in the picture spread of these products from pages 84 - 93.)

Join us in preparing dishes close to the hearts of the people of the region. May indigenous foods become a symbol of prosperity! **And may we treasure our traditions, our heritage.**

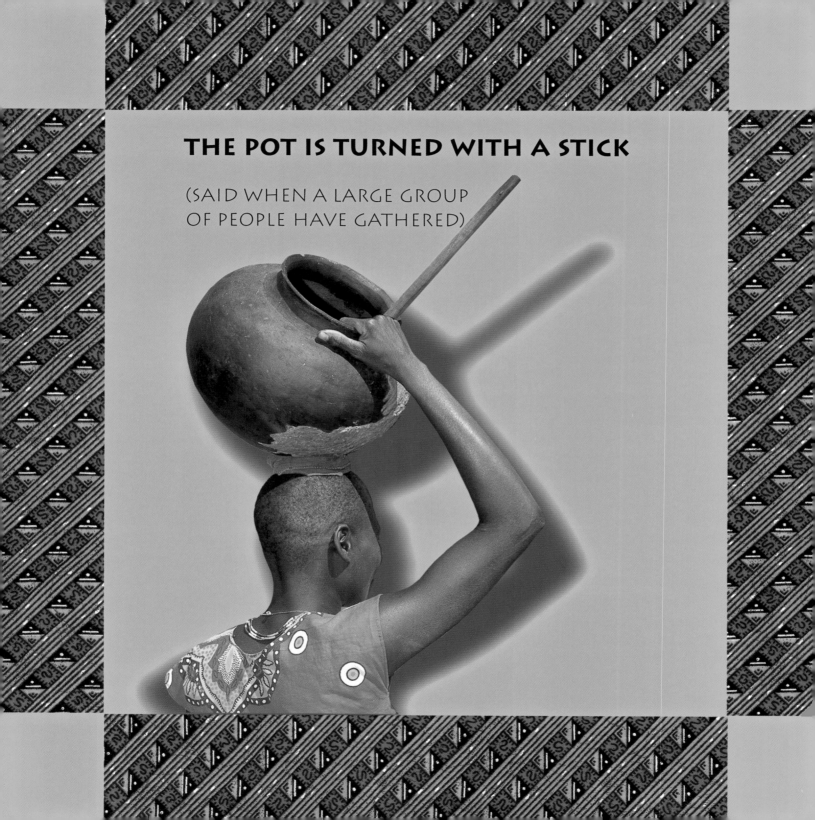

THE POT IS TURNED WITH A STICK

(SAID WHEN A LARGE GROUP
OF PEOPLE HAVE GATHERED)

INDEX

ACKNOWLEDGEMENTS

Women from rural South Africa, whose information and knowledge have been formalised in these recipes.

The Department of Science and Technology (previously the Department of Arts, Culture, Science and Technology) under the leadership of the Minister of Arts, Culture, Science and Technology, Dr Ben Ngubane. The Department's financial contribution is what has made this project possible.

Participating groups from all over South Africa

NORTH WEST
Bojanala Region
1. Itekeng-Group
2. Tsogang Madibeng
3. Lefatlheng
4. Seutelong Village
5. Stinkwater
6. Mogogelo
7. Mathibestad
8. Mmakau
9. Swartdam and Mmotla

Bophirima
1. Kelotso
2. Tirisano
3. Re-ba-Fenyi
4. Kgono
5. Batho Pele
6. Kgatelepelo
7. Kelotso
8. Lowe
9. Segarona
10. Re-a-Kgona

Central Region
1. Mmasuthe
2. Gaabo-motho-Traditional Food
3. Rapulane Traditional Food
4. Disaneng
5. Dithako East
6. Tlapeng
7. Bodibeng
8. Setlagole

Greater- Rustenburg Region
1. Kutiwano ke Maatla
2. Gomotsa Tlala
3. Kgobokgobo ya Ikgobokanyetsa
4. Re a Kgona
5. Kopano ke Tlimatla
6. Tsosanang
7. Letsatsi le Tlhabile
8. Tshwaraganang
9. A re direleng bomme
10. Bomme ba itireleng
11. Sogang le itireleng

The following organisations in North West:
- Entrepreneurial Support Centre (ESC)
- Department of Agriculture
- Participating municipalities

LIMPOPO
Western Region
1. Nkidikitlane project
2. Bogologolo
3. Hlatlolanang com. Project
4. Bopanang basadi
5. Mokgadi-women
6. Bogologolo
7. Remolokomo
8. Thabelane project

9. Mallokong
10. Hlanganang
11. Mabitsa Project
12. Harmabu
13. Arepheleng project
14. Arepheleng project
15. Motswiri
16. Mokgadi women

Northern Region
1. Mulendane Group
2. Thogani Group
3. Lwamondo Community Proj
4. Mabogo Poultry Project
5. Tlangelane
6. Matshavhawe Group
7. Pile Group
8. Tshivulane Community
9. Tshiopmbo group
10. Dzudza Cookery Group
11. Marandela
12. Budeli Group
13. Masakona Garden Group
14. Tshiombo Group
15. Thihangwi Sialala Group
16. Thengwe Group
17. Tshandama Group
18. Mukondeni Group

Lowveld-Giyani
1. Makhushane
2. Muyexe
3. Benfarm
4. Tlharihani
5. Tlakula
6. Tiyiselani
7. Namakgale
8. Makuwa
9. Hanyanya
10. Denser Settlement Project
11. Titirheleni
12. Mashishimale

The following organisations in Limpopo:
- Departments of Agriculture; Finance and Economic Development; Health
- Office of the Status of Women
- Office of the Premier
- Participating Municipalities

FREE STATE
Koffiefontein
1. Itekeng
2. Ipopeng
3. Tiisetsang
4. Bolokanang
5. Lesedi
6. Thusano
7. Helpmekaar
8. Ratanang
9. Reaiketsetsa
10. Zenzeleni
11. Vuka Bafasi

Botshabelo
1. Seya - le - methati
2. Ikaheng
3. Itumeleng
4. Iphahamiseng Trust
5. Fadimehang Project
6. Itshebeng Garden Project
7. Matlatsane Catering

Jagersfontein
1. Reaiketsetsa Project
2. Maholosiane
3. Helpmekaar
4. Tsoha o iketsetse
5. Ipopeng Sewing Group
6. Reteng

Bethulie
1. Ikaheng Group
2. Vuka u zenzele

Zastron
1. Ipopeng Poultry Project
2. Reaiteka Catering Project
3. Thusanang Burial Society

Thaba-Nchu
1. Leretlhabetse Group
2. Gladstone Village
3. Itsoseng Project

Virginia
1. Kopanang Batswadi
2. Phelang Bakery
3. Albany Sewing Group
4. Masivusane
5. Meloding Day Care Centre
6. Ikaheng Part 2

QwaQwa
1. Qenehelo Vegetable Project
2. Mamodiehi Sekeke
3. Matebello Mofokeng
4. Mantswaki Tladi
5. Seithati
6. Grass Project Traditional Healers
7. Fikapatso

The following organisations in the Free State:
- Mangaung University of the Free State Community Partnership Programme (MUCPP)
- Free State Business Resource Centre
- Departments of Tourism, Environmental and Economic Affairs; Sport, Arts, Culture, Science and Technology; Agriculture
- Participating Municipalities

KWAZULU-NATAL
North, North East, North West and South Region
Madlebe Ward
1. Siyathuthuka Youth
2. Sizamokuhle Club

3. Vuka mame Club

Kwa-Mbonambi and Madlanzini
1. Siphiwe ulwazi Club
2. Zimkeleni Club
3. Jazz Youth Club
4. Masakhane Club
5. Sicel' ulwazi

Sokhulu
1. Siyaphambili Club
2. Vusisiwe Club
3. Zisizeni Club
4. Sakhisizwe Club
5. Sidlangamandla Club
6. Zamokwethu Club

Siyakhona
1. Sicelamandla Youth Club
2. Mbabe Youth Club
3. Siyakhona Womens Club

Kwa-Bhejane
1. Khanyisani Club
2. Khenani Womens Club

Mevamphophe
1. Imbali Catering Club

Kwa-Mhlane
1. Ocilwane Youth Club
2. Siyakhona Club
3. Sicela' amandla Club
4. Ngwelezane

The following organisations in KZN:
- Andile Jordan and Associates
- Valley Trust
- Departments of Agriculture, Economic Development and Tourism, Health
- Durban Chamber of Commerce and Industry
- Rossing Nutritional Foods
- Zululand Chamber of Business Foundation
- Uthungulu District Municipality
- BHP Billiton

- Richards Bay Minerals
- DUMAC
- BCS Community Services
- University of Natal
- Business Linkage Centre
- Uthungulu Foundation
- Skills Dynamics
- Maputaland Information and Development Centre
- University of Zululand
- Mangosuthu Technikon
- Technikon Natal
- Hillside Aluminium
- Small Business Advice Centre

EASTERN CAPE
Port St. Johns
1. Golden Bowl
2. Hlamvana Women
3. Ecwebeni Women
4. Bholani Women
Amathole District
1. Rharabe Region
The following organisations in the Eastern Cape:
- Eastern Cape Appropriate Technology Unit (ECATU)
- Eastern Cape Development Corporation (ECDC)
- Department of Agriculture and Land Affairs
- Office of the Premier
- Municipality of Port St Johns

Fedics (Pty) Ltd

Traditional leaders of participating provinces
Dedicated staff of CSIR Food, Biological
and Chemical Technologies:
- **Technology for Development Programme**
- **Food Science and Technology Programme**
- **Investment and Business Development Programme**

Photography:
Darryn Brooks Photography, Eyescape Studios,
Proshots Photographics, Loretta Steyn Graphic
Design Studio, Rudi van Aarde.

Abner Nyamende,
for inclusion of his poem, *The Calabash*

REFERENCES

African Proverbs: Bagologolo ba re! Letöhama,
Creda Communications, Cape Town 1998

The Wisdom of the Tonga-Shangaan People, Henry Philippe
Junod and Alexandre A Jaques, The Central Mission Press,
Cleveland, 1935

Two Hundred and Sixty-four Zulu Proverbs, Idioms Etc and the
Cries of Thirty-Seven Birds, R.G. Dunning,
The Knox Printing and Publishing Company, Durban

African Wisdom, Ellen K Kuzwayo, Kwela Books, Cape Town
1998

Zulu Proverbs, C.L Sibusiso Nyembezi, Witwatersrand
University Press, Johannesburg 1974.

Poetry: Abner Nyamende

People's plants: A guide to useful plants in southern Africa.
Van Wyk, B and Gericke, N. 2000, Pretoria:
Briza Publications